Cosmicolour
COLOURING BOOKS

Teacup Critters

- AN ANIMAL COLOURING BOOK FOR ADULTS -

Before you start

We have provided a colour test chart on the following page for you to try out your medium of choice on our paper. For best results, we recommend that you only use coloured pencils or place a blank sheet behind each colouring page for all other mediums in order to prevent bleed-through.

We hope you enjoy this colouring book and look forward to seeing the masterpieces you create from it! To be featured on our social media pages use the hashtag #cosmicolourist when sharing your finished artwork. Be sure to also follow us for all the latest and more!

instagram.com/cosmicolouring
facebook.com/cosmicolouring

Colour test page

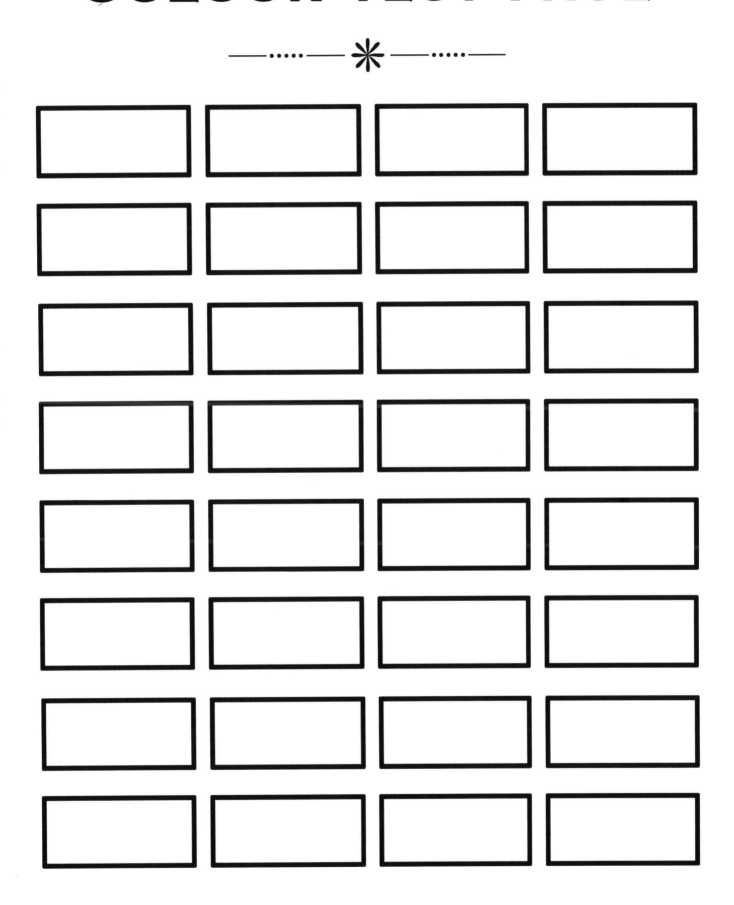